Mastering Basic

Preschool

Helping Children Succeed!

Table of Contents

What Color?

Color each picture.

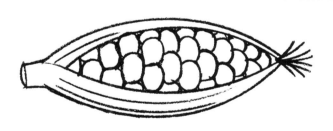 

Color Match

Color the pictures. Draw a line to match the colors.

Wacky Worm Patterns

Fill in the blank circles to continue each pattern.

Numbers 1 and 2

This is the number **1**.

Color **1** dog.

This is the number **2**.

Color **2** rabbits.

Who Needs What?

Draw lines to match the people to the objects they use.

 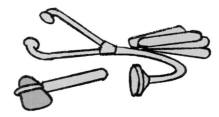

Numbers 3 and 4

This is the number **3**.

Color **3** turtles.

This is the number **4**.

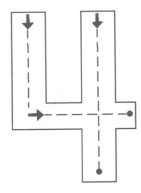

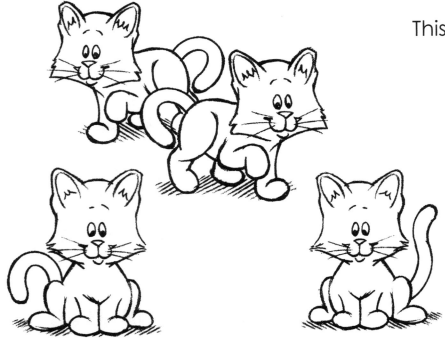

Color **4** kittens.

Finish Each Picture

Draw **1** scoop of ice cream on the cone.

Draw **2** eggs in the nest.

Draw **3** balloons for the girl.

Draw **4** fish in the pond.

Numbers 5 and 6

This is the number **5**.

Color **5** ducks.

This is the number **6**.

Color **6** raccoons.

Dot-to-Dot 1–6

Connect the dots from 1 to 6. What do you find?
Color the picture.

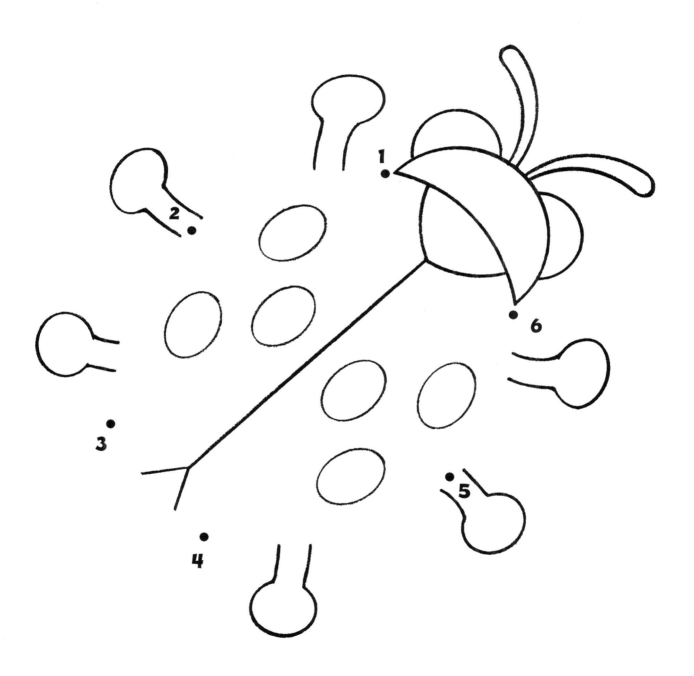

Numbers 7 and 8

This is the number **7**.

Color **7** owls.

This is the number **8**.

Color **8** mice.

Games and Activities: Colors

Muffin Pan Colors

Fill a muffin pan with water. Add a few drops of food coloring to each well to make red, blue, and yellow water. Give your child an eyedropper and a stack of white paper towels and let the discoveries begin. Have your child drop one color on the paper towel and then drop a second color on top of that. Watch as the two colors blend together to make a third color. For reference:

red	+	yellow	=	orange
red	+	blue	=	purple
yellow	+	blue	=	green

When your child is finished, allow time for the water on the paper towels to dry. Mount the colored towels on black paper and display them on your refrigerator.

Mixing Doughy Colors

This activity is a bit complicated but lots of fun. **You will need:** tempera paint or food coloring, Ivory soap flakes, a large mixing bowl, several small bowls (disposable paper bowls work very well), and self-sealing clear plastic sandwich bags. Mix up some Ivory soap flakes in the large bowl until the consistency is thick. Spoon a small amount of the white mixture into two bowls. Add a different color of food coloring to each bowl and mix well. Next, put a spoonful of each mixture into a self-sealing plastic bag. Let your child rub and squeeze the mixture until the two colors have formed a new color. Use the reference chart from the Muffin Pan Colors activity as a guide when making and mixing colors.

Yarn Pictures

Provide your child with six different colors of yarn: red, orange, yellow, green, blue, and purple. Have her dip the yarn into liquid starch or white glue, then place the yarn in the shape of a rainbow on light blue paper, representing the sky. Help your child complete the picture by creating clouds with cotton balls.

Color Wheel

Use a sturdy cardboard circle or an old pie tin for this activity. Divide the circle into eight sections and paint each section a different color. For each section of the circle, paint several clothespins the corresponding color. Your child will have fun identifying the colors as well as matching and then clipping the clothespins to the correct sections.

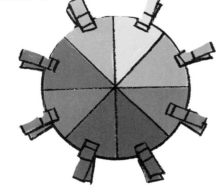

Match the Animal to Its Home

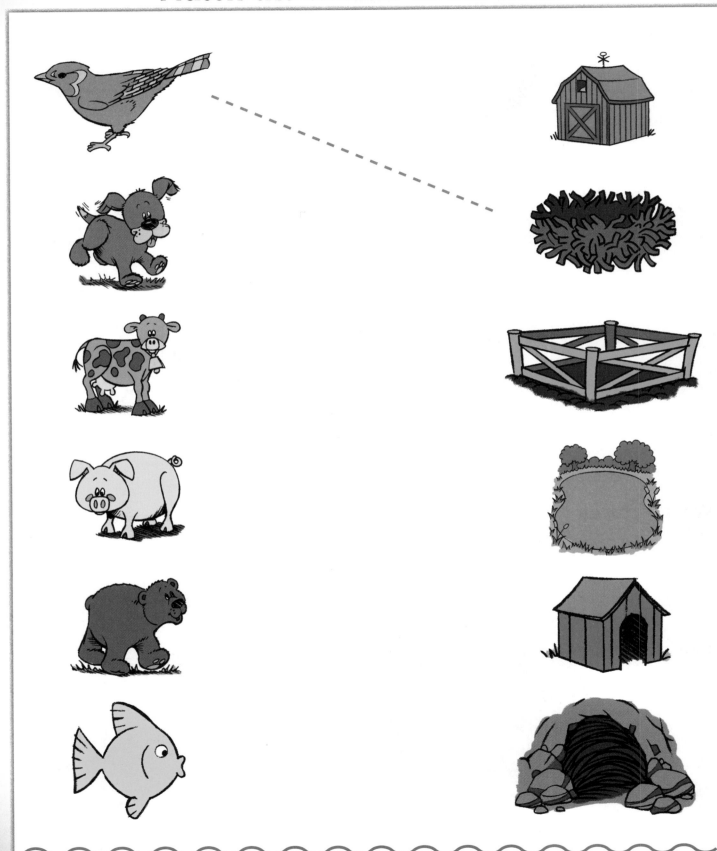

Letters Aa and Bb

Color the pictures that begin with the "**Aa**" sound.

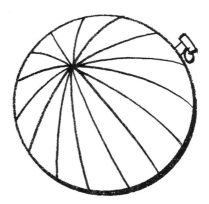

Color the pictures that begin with the "**Bb**" sound.

My Parents and Me: Play Dough Fun

"The Best" Play Dough

This is one of the best play dough recipes that can be made in your own kitchen. It is easy to make and will keep for weeks in a well-sealed plastic bag. **You will need:** 1 cup salt, 2 cups sifted flour, 2 tablespoons alum, 2 tablespoons vegetable oil, and 1 cup water. Mix all the ingredients together until they form a smooth mixture. Food coloring may be added to the water before it is poured into the mixture to add color. Children will spend hours enjoying the play dough they made all by themselves!

Make-Your-Own Clay Beads

You will need: 1 part cornstarch to 1½ parts flour and warm water, a mixing bowl, and a spoon. Add the warm water to the dry ingredients and mix to make a stiff dough. Dust with flour to prevent stickiness. Help your child roll the dough into the shape of a snake, then cut the long piece of dough into beads. Create holes in the beads with a nail. Allow the beads to dry. Your child will have fun stringing the beads with yarn and creating all sorts of interesting patterns.

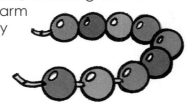

Magical Clay

This is one of the best recipes for making homemade clay that can be painted. Heat 2½ cups of water over low heat until you see bubbles. Remove the pan from heat. In a second pan, mix 1 cup cornstarch into ½ cup cold water until dissolved. Add the cornstarch mixture to the hot water and stir until the consistency is like clay. Form the clay into shapes or sculptures and allow the dough to dry at room temperature for three days. After 36 hours, the clay will become very hard and can be painted and sprayed with shellac.

Funny Putty

Funny putty is a crazy clay that is fun to make and incredibly fun to play with! This is one recipe that should be closely supervised, though, because it can get extremely messy. (Still, the fun is well worth the mess!) Add 2 parts white glue to 1 part liquid starch in a large plastic bowl. Mix well. If the putty is still too sticky after a couple of minutes, add more starch to make the mixture more workable. This funny putty has a really interesting texture. Your child may spend lots of time just squishing it in his hands. It is so much fun, you may want to play with it, too!

I Can Print My Name

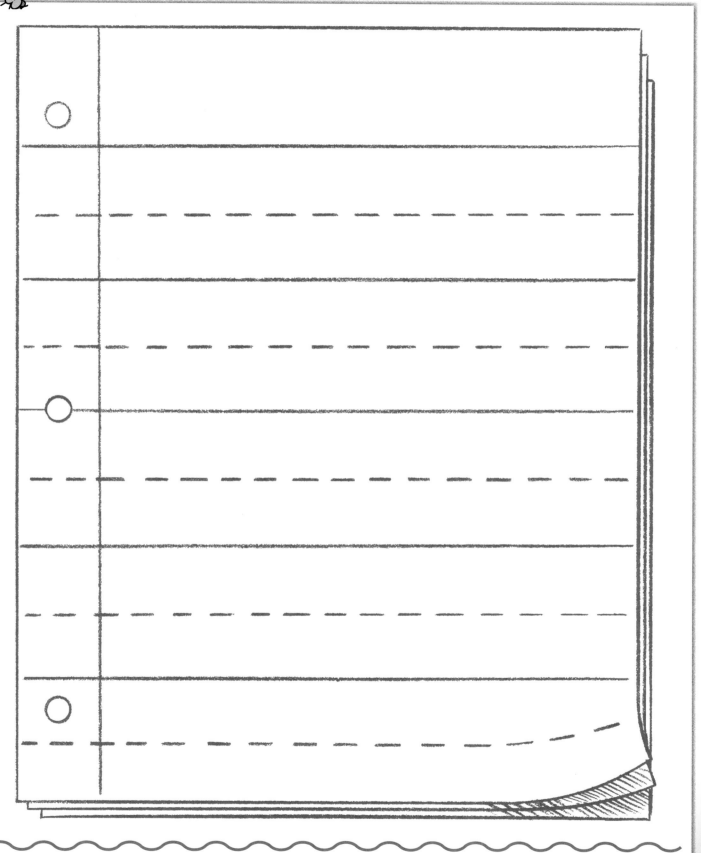

Seat Belts Keep Us Safe!

"Always wear your seat belt!"
That is a very important rule.
Remind your family to wear their seat belts.

Trace over the seat belts and color.

The Mice Go Marching

A "Read, Count, and Trace" Story

1

two

The mice go marching.
See number **2**?
He looks like a clown,
wearing those shoes.

3

three

The mice go marching.
Now I see **3**.
What's on her finger?
Buzz, her pet bee.

zero

one

The mice go marching.
Where did they go?
I don't see any.
Not one. **0**.

The mice go marching.
At last, there's **1**!
A cute little mouse,
sucking his thumb.

2

four

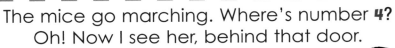
The mice go marching. Where's number **4**?
Oh! Now I see her, behind that door.

five

The mice go marching. There's number **5**.
He's dressed for the beach, ready to dive.

4

six The mice go marching. Wow, number **6**!
That lollipop's huge! You'll need two sticks!

seven The mice go marching. Here's **7**. Look!
What is she doing? Reading a book.

5

ten

The mice go marching.
Ten mice in all.
Look at **10**'s belly—
round as a ball!

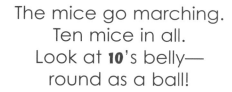

7

eight

The mice go marching. Watch number **8**.
She's running so fast, she must be late.

nine

The mice go marching. Hey, number **9**!
No need to worry. Just step in line.

6

Everyone's here now. Count them again!
And when you are through, that's it. **THE END.**

0   1   2   3   4   5

6   7   8   9   10

8

Letters Cc and Dd

C c

Color the pictures that begin with the "**Cc**" sound.

D d

Color the pictures that begin with the "**Dd**" sound.

Help the Chickens Cross the Road

Draw a line from the chicken to the coop.

Letters Ee and Ff

E 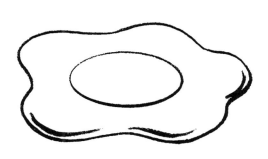 e

Color the pictures that begin with the "**Ee**" sound.

F  f

Color the pictures that begin with the "**Ff**" sound.

How Many Gum Balls?

Draw the correct number of gum balls in each machine.

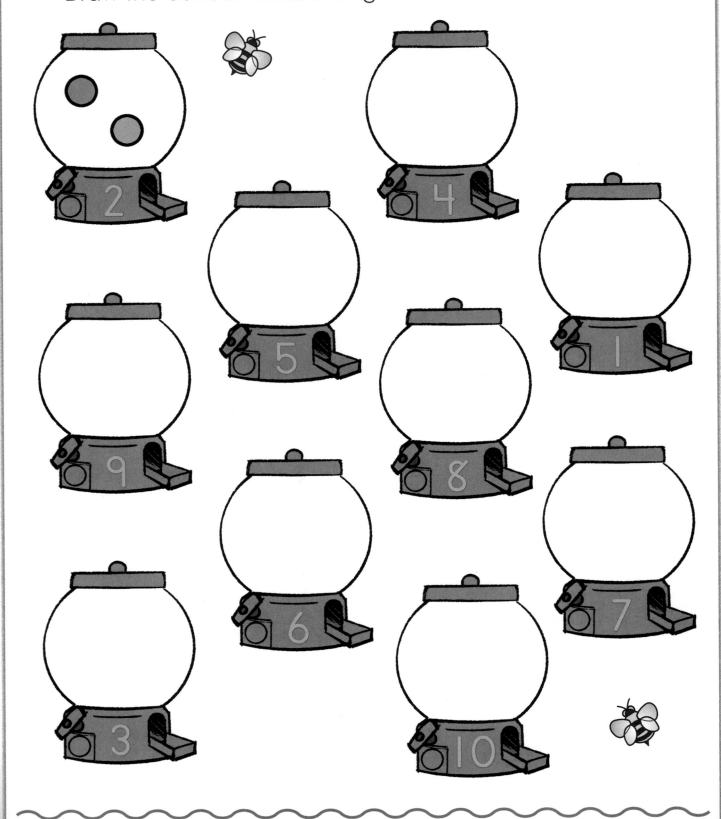

I Know My Telephone Number

Write your telephone number in the box.

Letters Gg and Hh

G G G G G G g g g

Color the pictures that begin with the "**Gg**" sound.

H H H H H h h h

Color the pictures that begin with the "**Hh**" sound.

Circle the Number 1-7

Count the number of objects in each row.
Circle the correct numeral.

  1 2 3 4 5 6 7

   1 2 3 4 5 6 7

    1 2 3 4 5 6 7

    1 2 3 4 5 6 7

 1 2 3 4 5 6 7

     1 2 3 4 5 6 7

Letters Ii and Jj

I i

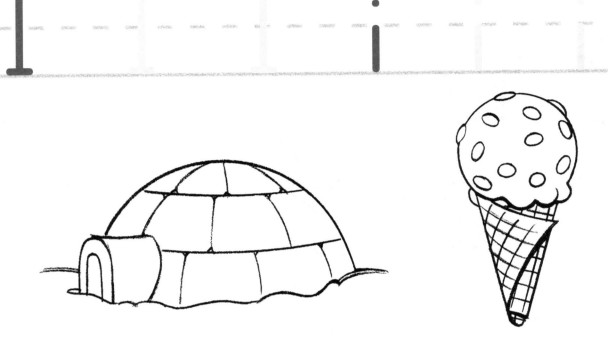

Color the pictures that begin with the "Ii" sound.

J j

Color the pictures that begin with the "Jj" sound.

Games and Activities: Learning to Print

Printing is a fine motor skill. Before young children are able to print properly, they need to strengthen and develop muscle control as well as eye-hand coordination. Developing these skills takes time and patience. You need to know that those first letter and numeral formations will be large, sometimes backwards, and often unreadable. That is normal at this stage in your child's development.

Before spending too much time teaching your child to print actual letters and numerals, spend some time on activities that strengthen pre-handwriting skills. You will find several activities that focus on fine motor skills in this book. These exercises will assist young children in developing some pencil control.

There are many other things you can do to help develop these skills, while also providing experiences that are successful and fun for your child. Try some of the ideas listed below.

Pre-Printing Ideas

- Give your child tracing and simple dot-to-dot activities to complete.

- Practice lines and circles (and letters or numerals if readiness is shown) on a sand-filled cookie sheet. The child can feel the shape and directionality of letters, numerals, lines, and circles.

- Finger paint is a wonderful medium for exploring the formation of shapes, letters, and numerals.

- Create play-dough, cookie, or bread-dough shapes, letters, and numerals. (It is also fun to bake and eat the ones made from cookie or bread dough.)

- Give your child a pair of scissors and several sheets of paper. With your supervision, have your child snip fringe all around the paper. This helps build fine motor muscles and increase fine motor control.

- Make shapes, letters, and numerals from small objects, such as buttons, small stones, pipe cleaners, string, and small blocks.

- Purchase stencils for your child. Playing with them will provide another experience to help develop eye-hand coordination and muscle control.

Note: If you are unable to tell if your child is right- or left-handed, do not encourage one hand or the other! Watch to see which hand your child uses most often. When handing your child a pencil, hold the pencil level to the middle of your child's midsection. Often children will take the pencil from an adult using the hand that is dominant.

See the numeral (page 65), uppercase alphabet (page 110), and lowercase alphabet (page 112) tracing pages for printing practice with letters and numbers.

Letter Pals

Match the uppercase letter to the lowercase letter.

A   • d

B   • a

C   • i

D   • e

E   • g

F   • b

G   • f

H   • c

I   • j

J   • h

Color the Pictures That Are the Same

Crossing the Street

Always cross the street with an adult.
Color the picture.

Read to your child: Cars move very fast. When you are little, it can be very dangerous to cross the street. I will teach you how to cross the street safely—then, when you are older, you will know how. But for now, you need to hold my hand.

Big and Little

Cut and paste the **big** things on the **big** toy chest.
Cut and paste the **little** things on the **little** toy chest.

Letters Kk and Ll

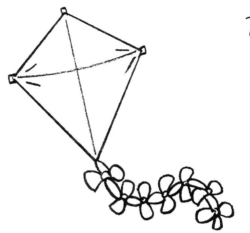

Color the pictures that begin with the "**Kk**" sound.

Color the pictures that begin with the "**Ll**" sound.

Games and Activities: Numbers

Two-Piece Number Puzzles

This is a wonderful self-checking activity that will seem more like puzzle play than math practice. Make a two-piece puzzle for each of the numerals 1 to 10 on 4" x 6" or 5" x 7" index cards or pieces of cardboard. On the left side of each card, put stickers to represent the numeral you have written on the right side. (See illustration.) Cut the cards in two, varying the design of each cut so that there is only one correct fit.

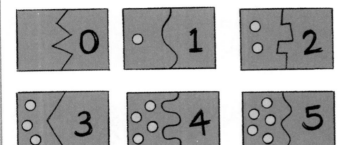

Two-piece puzzles are also effective for matching uppercase to lowercase letters, color words to colors, and photographs of family members to their names. The possibilities are endless.

File Folder Games

File folder games can be fun and educational. For this activity, make five to ten barns and glue them on the inside of a file folder. Label each barn with a numeral. Then, tape a clear plastic sandwich bag next to each barn, leaving the top open so animals may be put in the barn. Use farm animal stickers to make animals for the barns. Place the stickers on heavy paper (the top of a shirt box works well) and cut out. Prepare many animals. The goal for your child is to identify the numeral on each barn and place the correct number of animals in the bag next to the barn.

Try making other file folder games using paper planets and alien stickers, paper trees and apple stickers, or other fun combinations.

Number Jumping

This is a great rainy-day activity when your child needs active movement but cannot go outside. You will need an old plastic tablecloth or window shade. Using a permanent black marker, draw a path, a hopscotch grid, or a pond with stones on the tablecloth or shade. Label each section with a numeral. Have your child jump on the numbers in sequence, counting up, counting backwards, or counting by twos. Alternately, just have her jump on any number and say the name of that number out loud. This activity is also fun to do with beanbags. Have the child throw the beanbag and then tell you what number it lands on.

Shirt Box Counting

Make a lotto board on the inside bottom of a shirt box. (See illustration.) Make corresponding numeral cards from index cards. Have your child count the dots (or stickers) in each square and place the matching numeral card on top of that square. When your child is finished, simply put the numeral cards in the box, put on the cover, and the game is ready to store for use on another day.

Tracing Numbers 0-9

Practice writing each numeral.

Dot-to-Dot 1–10

Connect the dots from 1 to 10. Color.

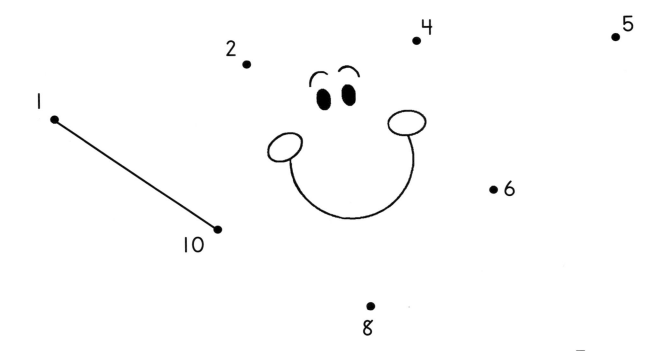

I Know My Address

Write your address on the lines.

Letters Mm and Nn

M M M M M M m m m m m

Color the pictures that begin with the "**Mm**" sound.

N N N N N N n n n n n

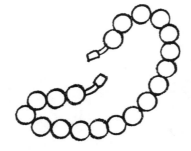

Color the pictures that begin with the "**Nn**" sound.

All about Me

Illustrated by

_____

(Your name)

1

This is my home.

3

This is what I looked like as a baby.

Some of my first words were:

_____

_____

_____

_____

_____

I was really cute.

This is my favorite food.

This is my favorite song.

This is my family. They love me and I love them.

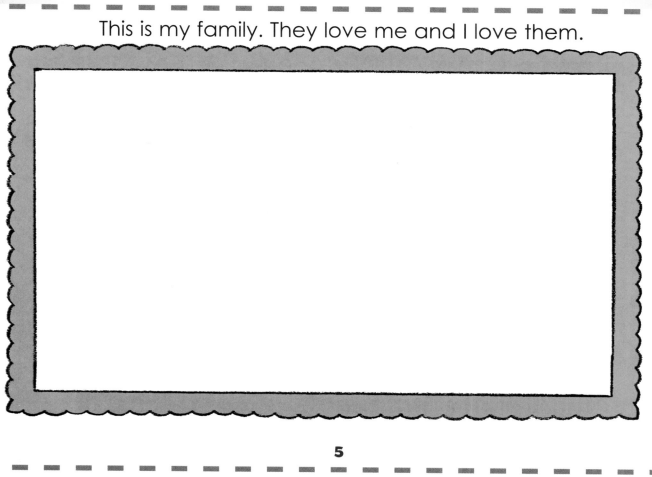

This is my favorite color.

This is my favorite animal.

This is my favorite TV show.

This is my best friend.

_____

(name)

6

This is my favorite toy.

This is what I want to be when I grow up.

I want to be a(n) _____.

8

Letters Oo and Pp

O  o

Color the pictures that begin with the "**Oo**" sound.

P P p

Color the pictures that begin with the "**Pp**" sound.

Bunnies Love Carrots

Help each bunny find its carrot.
Draw straight lines.

Up and Down

Cut out the bears.
Glue one bear climbing **up** the mountain.
Glue the other bear sliding **down** the mountain.

75

Color the Picture That Is Different

Letters Qq and Rr

 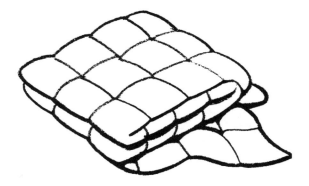

Color the pictures that begin with the "**Qq**" sound.

Color the pictures that begin with the "**Rr**" sound.

Games and Activities: Matching and Sorting

Matching and sorting are not just skills for young children—they are skills that everyone uses daily. Just think about it. How many times throughout the day do adults use these skills? We sort laundry by color and fabric; we sort dishes and silverware as we put them away; we sort money when we make budgets; we match what we record in our checkbooks to the bank statements; we match clothing to create outfits; we sort toys and other objects as we tidy our homes. Not only are these everyday life skills, but they are also important skills needed for mathematics and critical thinking.

Lots of Ways to Sort and Match

Here are several ideas to help your child develop necessary matching and sorting skills.

- Sort objects by color (pegs, buttons, cards, beads, blocks).
- Sort objects by shape (parquetry blocks, buttons, beads, seashells, animal crackers).
- Sort coins by color or value.
- Sort sounds as soft or loud.
- Sort toys as to where they belong when your child picks up her room.
- Sort clothes by type (shoes, shirts, shorts).
- Sort objects by function (tools, silverware, furniture).
- As your child becomes more skilled, begin sorting by two attributes, such as color and shape (red triangles, blue squares, yellow circles).

Egg Carton Sorting Box

An egg carton is a wonderful tool for sorting activities. Here are some examples of how to use one.

- Color the bottom of each egg section a different color. Have your child use the carton to sort a variety of things according to color.
- Print a numeral at the bottom of each section. Have your child place the correct number of objects in each section using a variety of objects.
- Glue buttons to the bottom of each section. Have your child sort according to the exact button or sort buttons according to color, shape, size, or number of holes.

Catalog and Magazine Activities

Catalogs and magazines are wonderful aids for creating matching and sorting activities. Here are just two examples of how to use them.

- Use two identical catalogs so you have access to identical pictures. Cut out two of the same picture and glue each onto an index card. Make several pairs of picture cards. Have your child match the identical objects or faces. Faces can also be sorted according to gender, age, and other categories.
- Using large catalogs, cut out pictures of things in particular categories, such as clothes, furniture, people, shoes, purses, luggage, things you use in the kitchen, things you use in the bathroom, and things that appeal to children. Glue onto index cards. Have your child sort the pictures into different categories.

Three Pigs and a Wolf

Show the pigs and the wolf to their homes.
Stay on the paths.

Over and Under

Cut and paste.
Put the birds **over** the mushroom.
Put the elf **under** the mushroom.

Letters Ss and Tt

S   s

Color the pictures that begin with the "**Ss**" sound.

T   t

Color the pictures that begin with the "**Tt**" sound.

Squirt Painting

This activity requires some bravery on the part of the parent, but your courage will be greatly rewarded when you see the delight on your child's face. Tape a large piece of paper (old newspaper works well) onto the trunk of a tree. Pour slightly watered-down tempera paint into a clean spray bottle (window cleaner bottles work well). To make this extra fun, prepare four or five spray bottles, each with a different color of paint. Then, let your child have fun spraying designs on the paper. The finished artwork may look as good as an original Jackson Pollock!

Driveway Chalk Drawings

Remember doing this when you were young? Well, now the chalk comes in more colors and in bigger sticks—perfect for little hands. Your child will have fun just drawing with chalk, but you can assist her in creating some driveway or sidewalk games as well. Draw pictures for your child to color. Have your child draw hopscotch grids, roads and towns for toy cars, or giant game boards where your child and friends can actually be the game pieces. Simply spending quality time playing with your child is the best thing a parent can do to ensure school success.

Large Murals

Children enjoy working on huge pieces of paper. Unroll a large sheet of wrapping paper or butcher block paper on the driveway or sidewalk and tape it in place. Give your child paints, chalk, crayons, and other materials to use to create a really big masterpiece. It is also fun to trace each other's outline. Trace your child's body and let him color in facial features and clothing. Then, let your child trace around your body and finish adding your features.

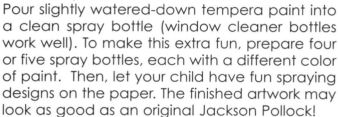

Rock Paperweights

Go on a nature hike and look for smooth rocks. The rocks you collect can be painted outside and then sprayed with shellac for a nice finish. Rock paperweights make excellent gifts for family members.

Colored Sand Jars

Your child can make some interesting designs using colored sand and a glass jar with a screw-on lid. (Colored sand can be purchased at most craft stores.) Help your child pour alternating colors of sand into a jar. The sand will stay in layers. Sand jars are pretty and interesting to look at. They also make a fun birthday party activity.

Sequencing 1, 2, 3

Cut out the pictures. Glue them on
the page in the correct sequence.

1.   2.   3.

A.   B.   C.

Letters Uu and Vv

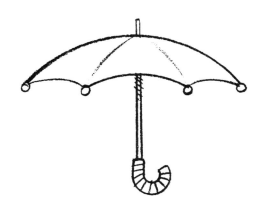 

Color the pictures that begin with the "**Uu**" sound.

Color the pictures that begin with the "**Vv**" sound.

Count and Circle

Count the objects in each row.
Circle the correct numeral.

1   3   4

2   4   3

5   2   1

2   1   4

1   5   3

Help the Bugs Get Home

Draw the path to each bug's home.

Patterning with Shapes

In each box, draw the shape that comes next.

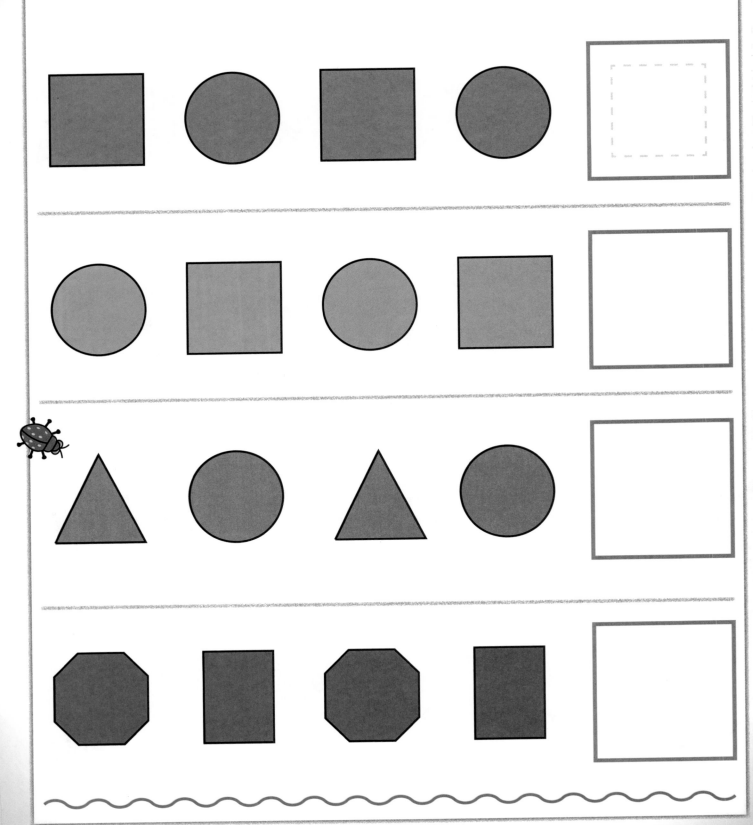

My Parents and Me: Creative Play Corners

Young children learn so much from imaginative play. They learn creativity as well as problem-solving skills. They build social skills and can acquire many pre-academic readiness skills, too. Here are some fun ideas for play corners that you and your child can create together.

The Hospital Corner

Doctors and nurses are favorite roles for children to play. Create a hospital environment in your own home with these simple ideas.

Medical equipment: Every medical professional needs a medical bag. You can create your own with an old black bag or purse. Add some bandages, tongue depressors, cotton balls, empty rubbing alcohol bottles, and straws, which make wonderful thermometers and syringes. Old trays can be used to display all the medical supplies in an operating room. You can make a stethoscope from a long piece of yarn and a small plastic or paper cup. Punch two holes in either side of the cup and string the yarn through the cup.

Uniforms and patients: Provide old white dress shirts for the doctors' and nurses' lab coats. Have several dolls and stuffed animals available to act as patients.

The Grocery Store

In order to create a great grocery store, there are some things you must first collect and prepare.

Food for the store: Save discarded containers, such as cans (be sure to clean and tape the raw edges); cereal and other food boxes; milk, egg, and juice cartons; and butter, margarine, and cottage cheese tubs. You will also want to purchase some plastic fruits and vegetables. Your child will have fun helping to decide what should be sold in the store.

Checkout items: For the checkout counter you will need a cash register or calculator, play money, grocery bags, aprons, and toy shopping carts. Not only will children have fun playing in the grocery store, but they will also learn about nutrition, the food groups, money, counting, and key concepts, such as top, middle, bottom, less, more, full, and empty.

The Dress-Up Corner

This is a favorite play area for many children, both girls and boys alike. Here are some suggestions for things you'll want on hand to make a fabulous dress-up corner: a mirror secured to a wall, a coatrack, briefcases, hats, shoes, wigs, purses, dresses, scarves, ribbons, aprons, jewelry, coats, dolls, sunglasses, old eyeglass frames (remove the lenses), makeup (if you are brave), badges, and boots. Almost anything you can think of to dress up in will be a welcome addition to this play corner. As the children play, listen to the language they use. You will be amazed by how far their imaginations can take them.

Things That Go Together

Draw a line to match the things that go together.

Letters Ww and Xx

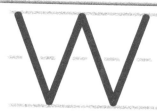

Color the pictures that begin with the "**Ww**" sound.

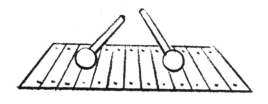 

Color the pictures that begin with the "**Xx**" sound.

Kangaroo Maze

Help the lost kangaroo find
her way to her friends.

Bees and Flowers

Use your pencil to help the bees find their flowers.

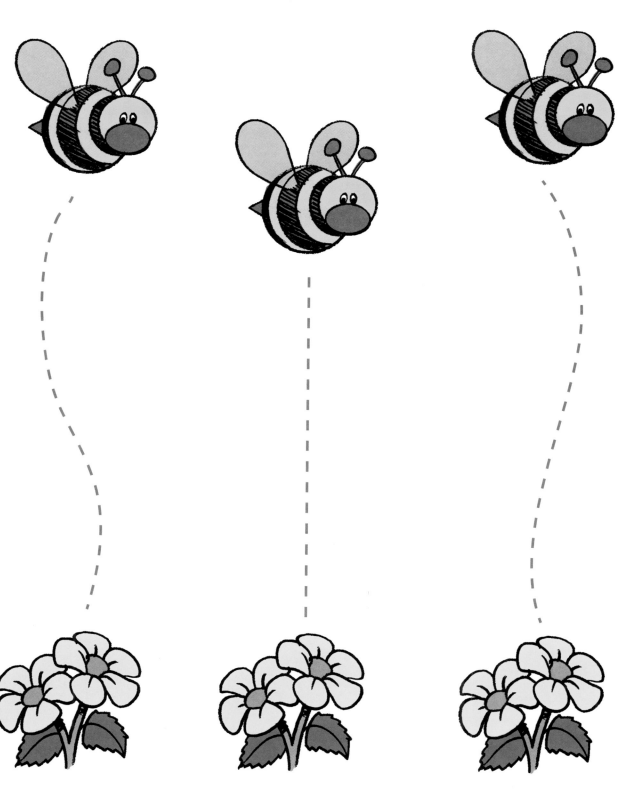

Letters Yy and Zz

Color the pictures that begin with the **"Yy"** sound.

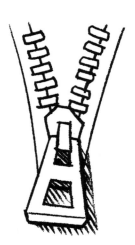

Color the pictures that begin with the **"Zz"** sound.

I Can Read My ABC's

A "Trace and Color" Book

1

E is for

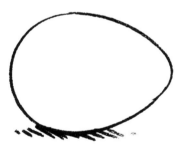

F is for

G is for

H is for

3

A is for

B is for

C is for

D is for

2

I is for

J is for

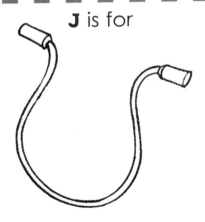

K is for

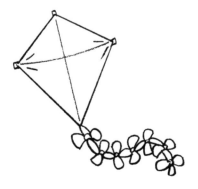

L is for

4

M is for

N is for

O is for

P is for

5

U is for

V is for

W is for

X is for

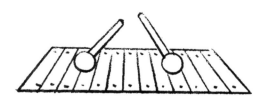

7

Q is for

R is for

S is for

T is for

6

Y is for

A-B-C-D-
E-F-G-
H-I-J-K-
L-M-N-O-P-
Q-R-S-T-U-V-
W-X-Y and Z.

Z is for

Now I know my **ABC**'s. Next
time won't you
sing with me?

8

Mother and Baby Memory Match

Cut out the cards. Spread them out facedown. One player turns over two cards. If the cards show a mother and baby animal match, the player keeps the cards and takes another turn. If the cards do not match, the player turns the cards back over, and the next player takes a turn.

Traffic Light

Color the traffic light.

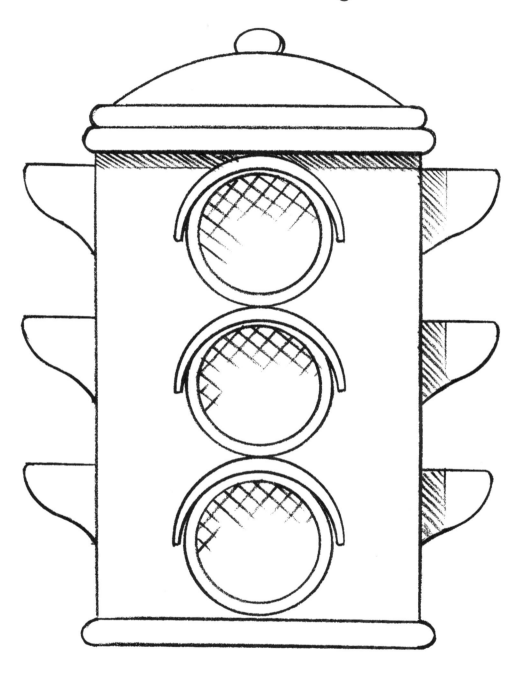

Red on top means you must **stop!**
Green below means you may **go!**

My Parents and Me: Cooking Fun

Ice Cream Clown

This fun dessert is a special treat that young children will love! Place one scoop of ice cream on a plate. Put a cone on top of the ice cream for a hat. Add candy-covered chocolates for eyes, a cherry for the nose, and chocolate chips for the mouth. If desired, decorate the cone hat with whipped cream.

Frozen Bananas

Sometimes it is difficult to convince a young child that it is good to eat healthy snacks. Here is a fun idea that will persuade your child to eat a treat that is also nutritious. Peel a ripe banana and push a clean craft stick into one end. Dip the banana into a mixture of ½ cup water and ½ cup lemon juice to prevent discoloring. Roll the dipped banana in any combination of the following toppings: chopped nuts, melted chocolate, sesame seeds, wheat germ, or cinnamon. Set the banana on wax paper and freeze for at least one hour before eating.

Edible Necklaces

Give your child an 18" piece of yarn with masking tape wrapped around each end. The masking tape will serve as a needle. Let your child string pieces of cereal, candy, or any other small foods that have holes in the middle. Your child will enjoy wearing and munching on the edible necklace.

Tiny Pizzas

Tiny pizzas are easy to make and provide a warm, fun-to-eat lunch. Split an English muffin in half. Spread 1 tablespoon spaghetti sauce on each half. Add slices of pepperoni or other favorite toppings. Sprinkle with shredded mozzarella cheese and a dash of oregano. Place in the oven or toaster oven at 425°F until the cheese melts.

Terrific Trail Mix

If you are the parent of a young child, it is a good bet that your pantry is filled with nearly empty boxes. Use these items to create your own trail mix. Mix together in a storage bag small amounts of cereal, raisins, sunflower seeds, peanuts, pretzels, and other goodies. Serve in small paper cups.

Ham and Cheese Roll-ups

You will need: 1 can refrigerated crescent rolls, 2 cups chopped ham, 1 cup shredded cheddar cheese, butter, a knife, measuring cups, and a cookie sheet. Flatten each crescent roll on the cookie sheet. Spread butter over the center, sprinkle with ham and cheese, and roll up, starting with the wide end. Bake at 400°F for 10 to 12 minutes. This recipe will make eight ham and cheese roll-ups for a fabulous lunch.

Top and Bottom

Cut and paste.
Put the blocks on the **top** shelf.
Put the drum on the **bottom** shelf.

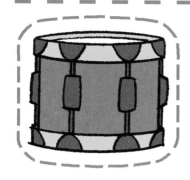

What Does Not Belong?

In each box, draw an **X** on the picture that does not belong.

Dot-to-Dot A–Z

Connect the dots from **A** to **Z**.
Color the finished picture.

On the Farm

Count the farm animals.

How many?

Count the animals
you see on the farm.

Write the correct
number next to
each animal.

Tracing My Uppercase ABC's

Trace each letter of the alphabet.

First and Last

Circle the thing that happened **first**.
Draw an **X** on the thing that happened **last**.

Tracing My Lowercase ABC's

Trace each letter of the alphabet.

Stay Away from Strangers

Strangers are people that you do not know. Do not talk to strangers, and never go anywhere with someone you do not know. Always stay near your parents or the people your parents have asked to take care of you.

Color this child. He is smart.
He knows not to talk to or go anywhere with a stranger.

Circus Circles

It's a three-ring circus!
Trace the rings.

Super Safety Kid

A "Read, Write, and Do" Story

I WANT YOU TO KNOW WHAT TO DO!

1

Super Safety Kid says: **"K**NOW YOUR TELEPHONE NUMBER."

You can always call home if you know your telephone number.

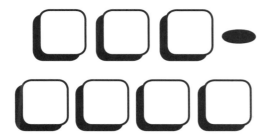

Print your telephone number.

Practice punching in your phone number on a calculator.

3

Super Safety Kid says: **"SMART PEOPLE WEAR SEAT BELTS."**

Draw in the seat belts.

Sometimes adults forget to use their seat belts. **Remind them!**

2

Super Safety Kid says: **"BRING AN ADULT WITH YOU WHEN YOU CROSS THE STREET."**

Cars move **too fast** and sometimes drivers cannot see you! Someday, when you are older, you will be able to cross the street alone.

4

Super Safety Kid says: "**K**NOW YOUR ADDRESS."

Ask your mom or dad to print your address.

_____

_____

_____

You can always find home when you know your address!

5

Can you say it by yourself?

Super Safety Kid says:

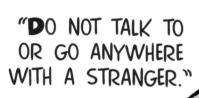 "**D**O NOT TALK TO OR GO ANYWHERE WITH A STRANGER."

 NO!

Never talk to strangers, and never go with any adult that does not know your family's secret password. Passwords are only given to people that your mom and dad know are safe.

Parents: Give your child a password—something special your child will not forget. Only people who know the password are allowed to pick up your child. Everyone will feel more secure.

7

Super Safety Kid says:

"RED ON TOP MEANS YOU MUST STOP.
GREEN BELOW MEANS YOU MAY GO."

Color the lights .
What does yellow mean?

STOP

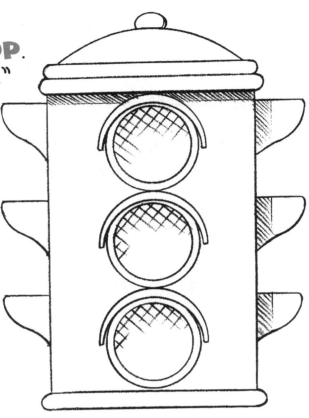

6

Super Safety Kid says:

"DIAL 911
WHEN YOU NEED
HELP."

911

911

8

More or Less?

Circle the container that has **more.**   Circle the container that has **less**.

My Parents and Me: Painting Fun

Pudding Paint

Sometimes painting is more fun when you use something other than paint. Next time, try pudding! Mix regular instant pudding in a large jar with a tightly sealed cap. Children love shaking the jar to thicken the pudding. Chill until the pudding is set. Spoon pudding onto a clean counter or kitchen table and let your child finger paint (and snack on the pudding, too!).

Shaker Painting

Mix equal parts tempera paint and salt in a salt or spice bottle. Do not add water. Have your child create designs on a piece of construction paper with white glue. Shake the powdered paint mixture over the glue design and let dry. Once the glue has dried, gently shake off any extra salt crystals to reveal the masterpiece.

Cotton Swab Painting

Young children often have trouble controlling a paintbrush and large amounts of paint. Here is a fun idea that helps to control the mess and provides children more control with the paint. Fill an old ice tray with liquid tempera paint or use watercolors. Give your child a cotton swab for each color and let him have fun painting. You will find that this painting experience is less of a mess. Simply throw away the swabs when the painting is completed.

Make Your Own Finger Paint

This finger paint recipe is easy to make and provides a fun tactile experience. Mix together 1 cup flour, 1½ teaspoons salt, 1 cup sand, and 1 cup water. Add food coloring or paint for color. You may also switch the proportions of salt and sand, if desired.

Soapy Paint

Mix together Ivory soap flakes and a small amount of water until you have created the consistency of whipped cream. Then, add powdered tempera paint or food coloring. This is a fun finger paint to use on a smooth tabletop or on finger paint paper. The soap flakes make for easy cleanup.

Special Note: *Before you let your child paint all over your table or countertops, please try the paint on a corner. The paint generally cleans up easily, but it never hurts to double-check that you are not coloring your countertops permanently.*

Slip and Slide

Trace the path down the hill with your pencil.
Be careful!

Decorate Dad's Ties

Draw the correct number of dots on each tie.

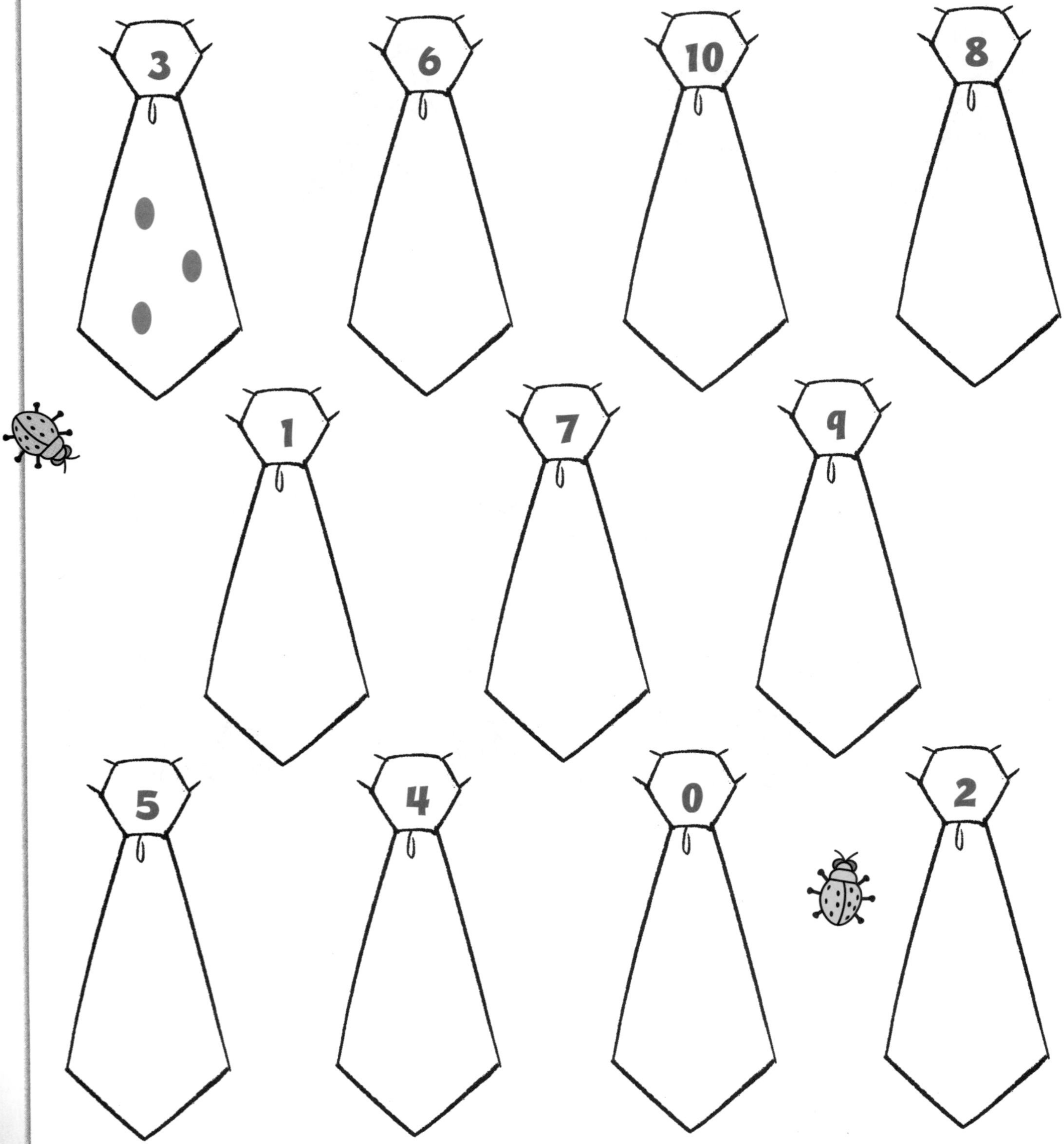

3

6

10

8

1

7

9

5

4

0

2

Food Groups

Color, cut, and sort according to food groups.

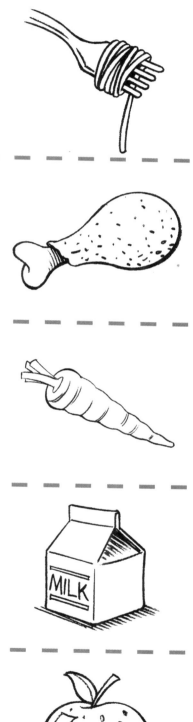

Games and Activities: The Five Senses

I Can See

Have your child make a set of binoculars. **You will need:** two toilet paper tubes, yarn, and two paper clips, brads, or tape. Attach the two tubes side by side with the clips, brads, or tape. Punch a hole in each tube and add a piece of yarn so the binoculars can be worn

around the neck. Take your child on a nature hike and let her investigate with the binoculars.

I Can Feel

Make a texture memory match game.

- **You will need:** 20 or more empty thread spools or small wooden blocks, glue, and a variety of textures, such as sandpaper, wool, silk, velvet, flocked wallpaper, crumpled foil, yarn, and cotton balls.

Cut small pieces of the materials and glue them onto the spools or blocks. Make two with each material. Your child will enjoy feeling the different textures and trying to match the identical ones. This is especially fun with closed eyes.

Note: *Do not use a blindfold. Having something tied over the eyes is often scary for a preschooler or kindergartner.*

- Fill a bag with various textures. Have your child close his eyes, reach in the bag, pull out a material, and describe it as either "smooth" or "rough."

I Can Hear

If you do not already own a tape recorder, you may want to get one. Tape recorders can provide hours of fun and learning.

- Record your child talking or singing into the tape recorder and play it back. Children delight in hearing how they sound.

- Record several everyday sounds: phone ringing, clock ticking, vacuuming, water running, dog barking, and so on. Play the tape for your child and have her identify the sounds.

- Record yourself reading some of your child's favorite stories. Your child can pretend to read along. This tape might also be useful on nights when you are out and your child has a baby-sitter.

- Record yourself reading a story and have your child do the sound effects or say the repetitive lines, such as "I'll huff, and I'll puff, and I'll blow your house down!"

Special Note: *The next two senses have been downplayed because it is so important that young children learn not to smell or taste anything that the parents or another responsible adult has not given the child.*

I Can Taste and Smell

When cooking, have your child sample a variety of foods. Use descriptive words to talk about how things taste. Sampling different foods may encourage better eating habits in a fussy eater. Point out various smells in the house, when on nature walks, and in other situations where strong smells are present. Be sure to stress the above special note with your child.

See and Hear

Color the things you can **see**.

Color the things you can **hear**.

Inside and Outside

Draw a circle ◯ around the things you find **inside**.
Draw a square ☐ around the things you find **outside**.

Taste, Smell, and Touch

Color the things you can **taste**.

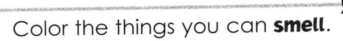

Color the things you can **smell**.

 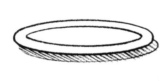  

Color the things you can **touch**.

The Birds Are Lost

Trace the path from each bird to its nest.

My Parents and Me: I Love My Grandparents

Special Dinner for Grandparents

Invite your child's grandparents over for a special dinner. Let your child decide on the menu and help prepare the dinner. Prepare whatever your child wants, whether it be hot dogs and pudding or peanut butter sandwiches! Grandparents will love the fact that their grandchild has planned this special evening, and your child will have the wonderful memory of giving his grandparents this special gift.

Family Tree

This family tree project makes a wonderful gift for grandparents; it also provides the opportunity to teach your child some family history. Make a tree out of construction paper. Glue it onto a paper plate. Frame your child's picture and glue it to the center of the plate on top of the tree. Let your child glue pictures of family members all around the plate. As you are working on this project, discuss how each family member is related and how each of them loves your child. When the project is completed, wrap it up and let your child present it to her grandparents. Your child can have the fun of explaining all that she learned about your family while making the gift.

Picture Paperweight

Paperweights are easy to create and make great gifts. You will need: a photo of your child, a clear plastic cup, felt, plaster of Paris, and glue. Trim the photo so that it fits into the bottom of the cup. Squeeze a small amount of glue into the bottom of the cup and press the picture facedown onto the glue. Let dry overnight. Check to see if it is ready by looking at the photo. All the glue should have dried clear and the photo should be easily seen. Mix the plaster of Paris according to the directions, pour into the cup, and let dry completely. The plastic can then be cut away from the cup. Glue a piece of felt to the bottom of the paperweight so that it does not scratch furniture. This picture paperweight is truly a gift to be remembered.

My Picture of Grandma and Grandpa

There is nothing more adorable than the artwork of a young child. Ask your child to draw a picture of his grandparents. Encourage details, but do not assist with the drawing. When your child is finished, frame the piece of art and help your child wrap the gift. Grandparents will be thrilled to receive the gift! Your child will also be thrilled to have made something that is so treasured!

On and Off

Cut and paste.
Put one guinea pig **on** the block
Put the other guinea pig **off** the block.

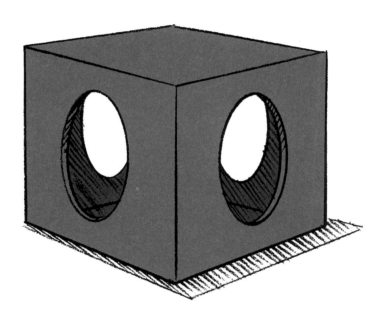

Count and Color 1-10

Trace the number. Color the correct number of objects in each row.

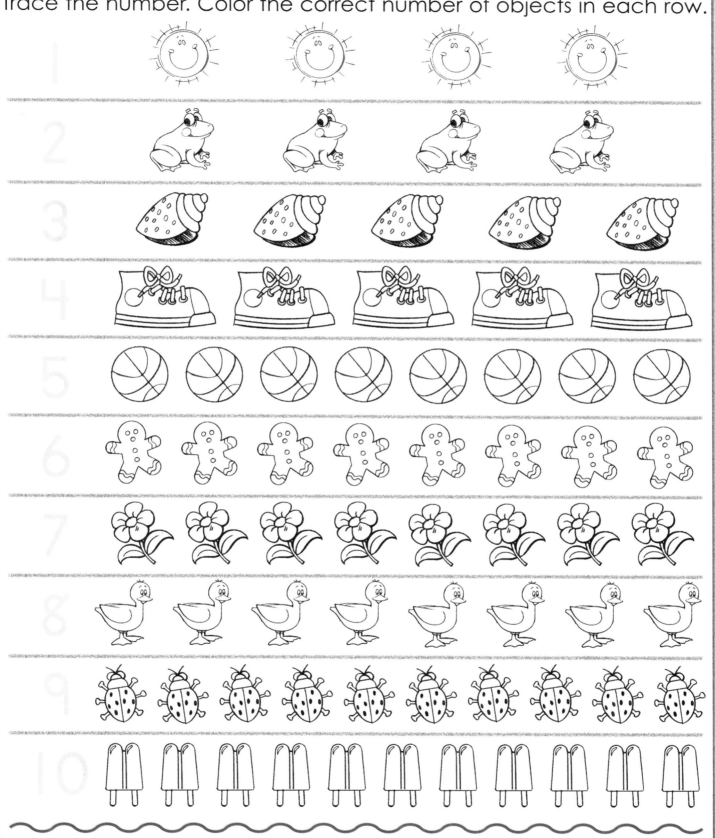

Animal Match

Match each mother to her baby.

Let's Drive!

Draw a straight line to drive each car into its garage.

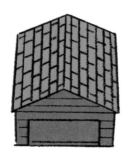  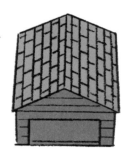 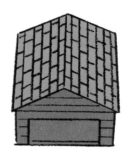

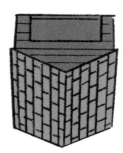 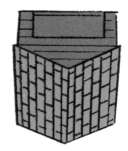 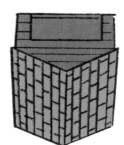 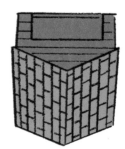

How Many in Each Box?

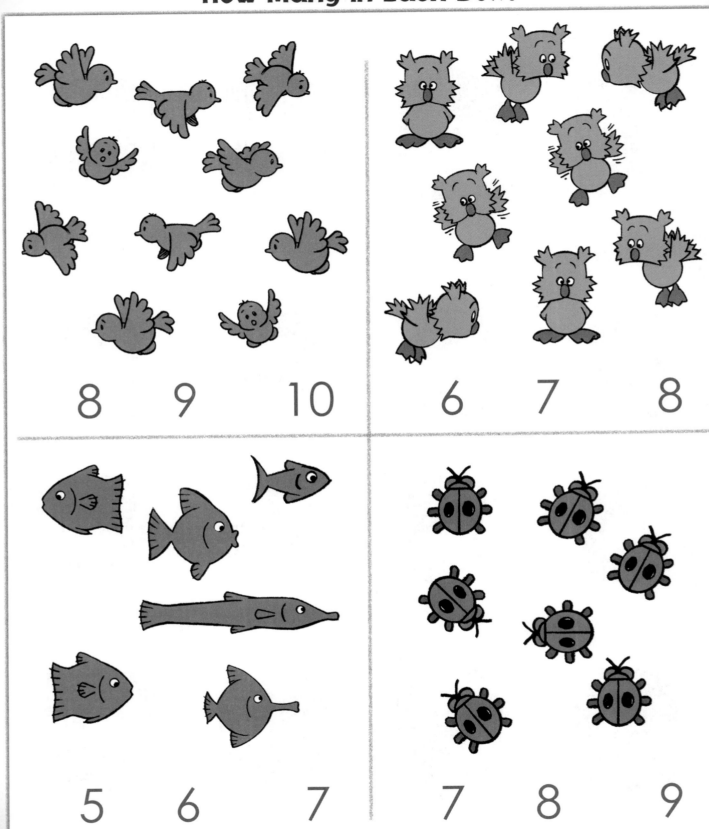

8   9   10

6   7   8

5   6   7

7   8   9

Day and Night

Cut and paste.
Put the pictures of **day** under the sun.
Put the pictures of **night** under the moon.

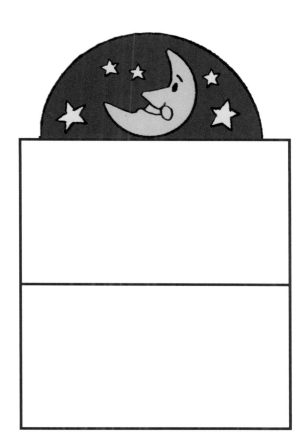

My Parents and Me: Family Fun

Here are four fun activities that families will enjoy doing together.

Balloon Catch

Young children (and adults) always seem to enjoy playing with balloons. Here is a fun family idea for playing catch with balloons.
For this version of catch, you will need a balloon and funnels. If you do not have funnels, you can easily make them by rolling pieces of tagboard into funnel shapes. Tape each funnel to a tongue depressor and give one to every player. One person (usually the youngest) starts the game with the balloon on her funnel. That player pushes the funnel up to toss the balloon. The other player or players try to catch the floating balloon on their funnels. Count out loud to see how many times you can keep the balloon up in the air. This is a great activity for increasing eye-hand coordination.

Paper Airplanes

Nearly everyone has made and flown a paper airplane at least once. There is something magical about watching a plane fly through the air. Take your child outside to fold and fly paper planes. Guess how far each plane will fly. Whose plane will fly the lowest? Whose plane will fly the farthest? Whose plane will fly the highest? Whose plane will fly the fastest? Just think of all the wonderful concepts (and the idea of estimation) that can be taught simply by flying paper airplanes!

Creepy Crawler Can

Young children love pretending that they are explorers. Help your child make a creepy crawler can to take with him on his next adventure. Use a cylindrical cardboard oatmeal container as the can. Cut out a section for the window. Tape screen or netting to the inside of the box to cover the window. Punch holes on either side of the container near the top and attach a string for a handle. (See illustration.) Now, go on a hunting adventure and see what you can catch!

Note: Remember to be gentle and release everything you have caught.

Gigantic Bubbles

In order to make huge bubbles, you will need a large bottle of bubble solution, a wire hanger or long piece of heavy wire, and a pizza pan. Bend the hanger or wire into a circle, using the hook as a handle. Pour the bubble solution into the pizza pan. Dip the circular part of the hanger into the solution and wave quickly through the air in a big circle. Watch as the gigantic bubbles appear. You can also make your own bubble solution. Mix together 1 gallon cold water and 1 cup liquid detergent. Let sit overnight in a cool place. Add 2 tablespoons liquid glycerin. Enjoy watching the terrific bubbles you and your child made together.

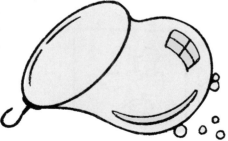

Trace the Circles and Squares

Trace the **circles**.

Trace the **squares**.

Color the Circles and Squares

Color the s.

  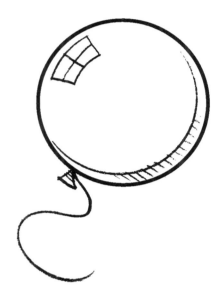

Color the s.

  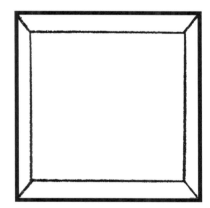

Trace the Triangles and Rectangles

Trace the **triangles**.

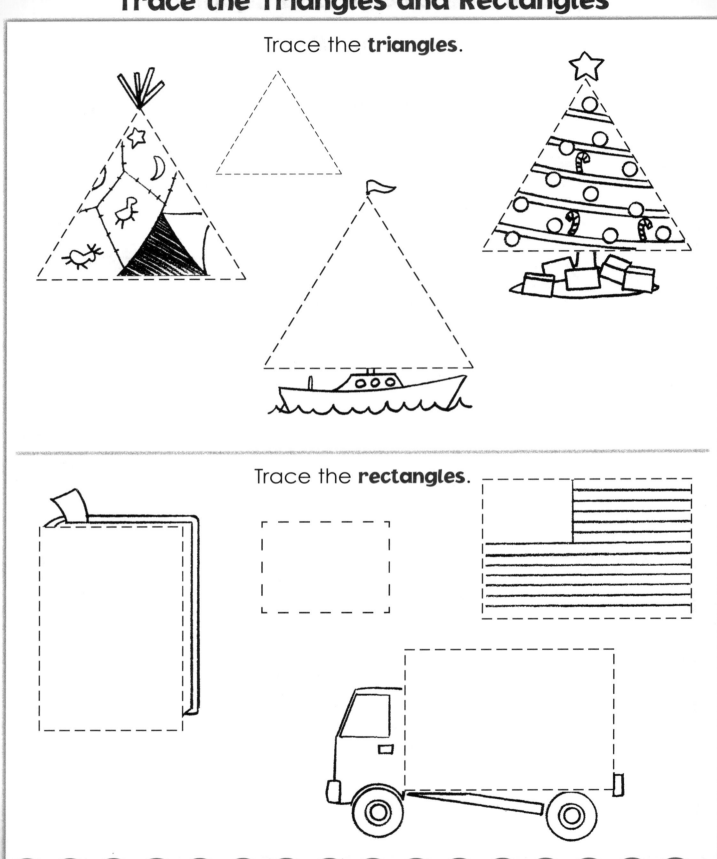

Trace the **rectangles**.

Color the Triangles and Rectangles

Color the ▲ s.

Color the ■ s.

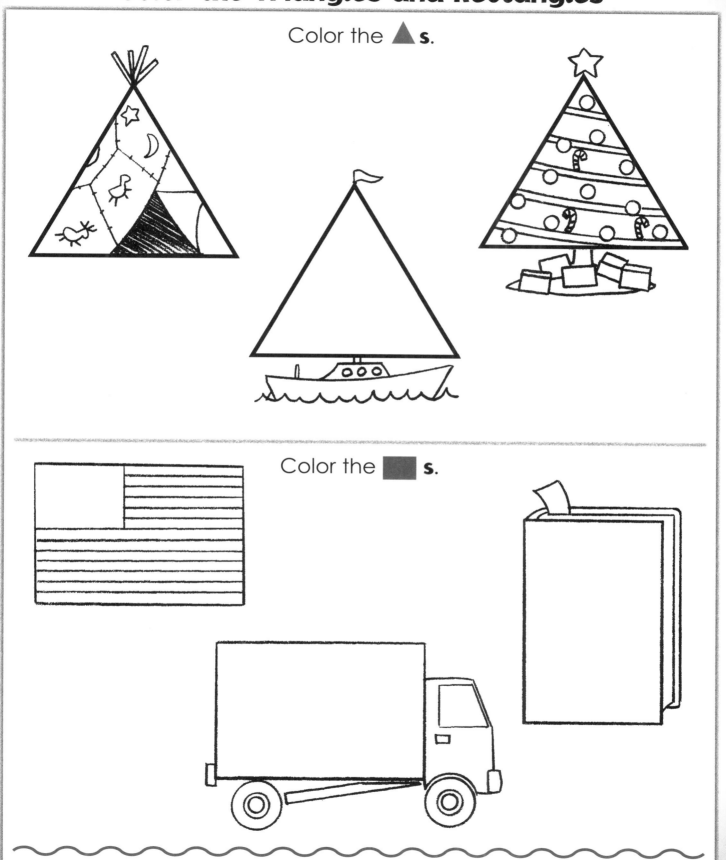

Trace the Stars and Diamonds

Trace the **stars**.

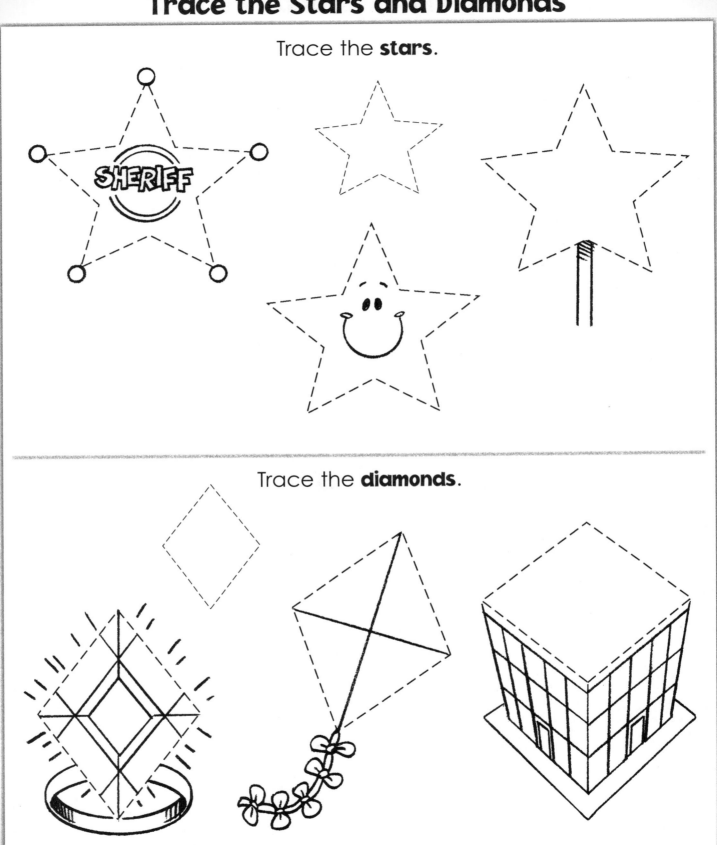

Trace the **diamonds**.

Color the Stars and Diamonds

Color the 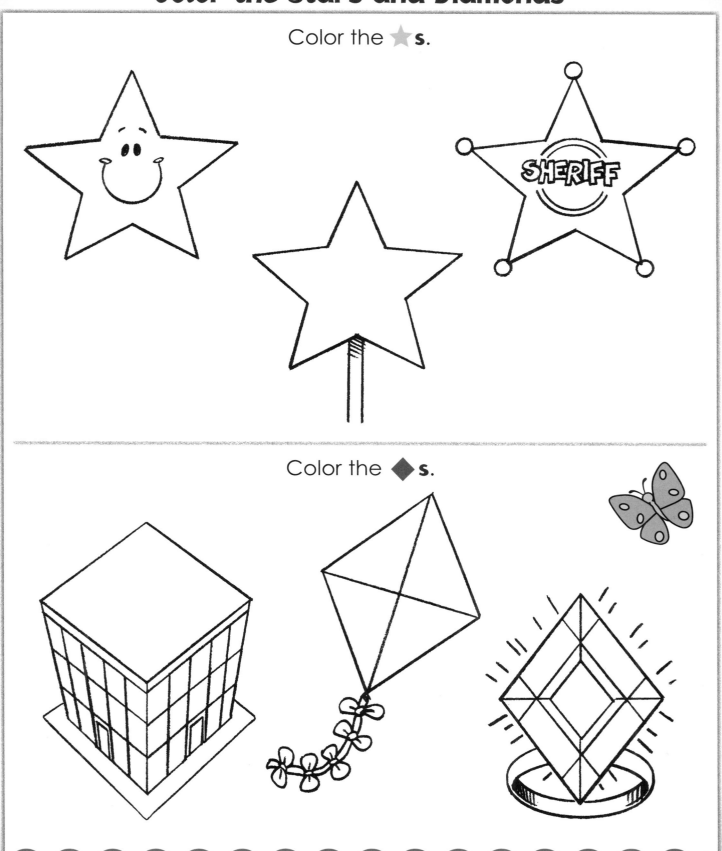s.

Color the ◆s.

Games and Activities: Shapes

Artistic Shapes

There are many ways for you and your child to make shapes that will allow your child to touch and feel the actual forms. Multisensory learning 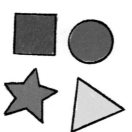 can be a powerful teaching tool for a young child. Not only does the child see the shape and verbally identify it, but also recognizes the shape by the way it feels. Here are some fun ideas for creating touchable shapes.

- **Play-Dough Shapes.** Use any of the play-dough recipes found on page 42. Make the dough and then have fun forming the shapes.

- **Dot-to-Dot Shapes.** Make a dot-to-dot shape on a piece of paper. Instead of using a pencil, have your child use white glue to connect the dots. When the glue is dry, the child can trace a finger over the solid glue and feel the shape.

- **Yarn Pictures.** Dip pieces of colored yarn in white glue. Arrange the yarn on a sheet of construction paper. When the glue is dry, your child can feel the shape by touching the yarn.

- **Shape Collage.** Using a variety of colors of construction paper, pre-cut for your child a multitude of paper shapes. Let your child create a collage by gluing the shapes onto a large piece of construction paper.

Beanbag Shape Board

If you or another family member is handy with construction materials, try creating this easy-to-make game that will last for years. Simply cut a variety of shapes out of one piece of plywood. (See illustration.)

Mount a stand on the back of the plywood, and purchase or make some beanbags. Children love throwing things at a target and can practice naming the shapes as they aim their beanbags.

Fishing for Shapes

The traditional game of fishing with a magnet is loved by all children. Make a simple fishing pole from a yardstick, meterstick, or dowel rod. Attach a magnet to one end of the pole with a long piece of string. Cut out several construction paper fish. Draw a shape (or color, number, alphabet letter, etc.) on each fish and attach a paperclip. Throw the fish in a cardboard box pond and go fishing. Make up games as you fish. Maybe you only want to catch the "star" fish, so all others have to be thrown back; maybe the triangle fish are dangerous, so extra caution must be taken; or maybe the circle fish are good luck, so they earn you an extra turn!

My Own Felt Shapes

Glue a piece of black felt on the inside cover of an old cardboard pencil box. Cut out felt shapes in a variety of colors. These shapes can be stored inside the box. Your child will have tons of fun making pictures with the shapes on the black felt background. Add felt numbers, colors, and letters to the box for added enrichment.

Above and Below

Cut and paste.
Paste one rocket **above** the moon and stars.
Paste one rocket **below** the moon and stars.

Trace the Ovals and Octagons

Trace the **ovals**.

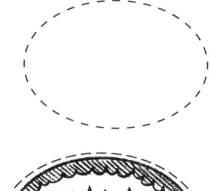

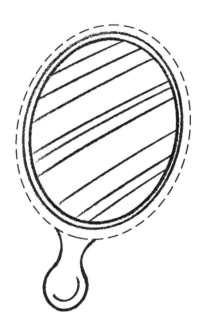

Trace the **octagons**.

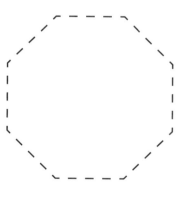

Color the Ovals and Octagons

Color the s.

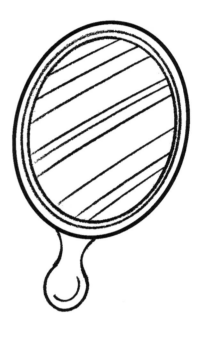

Color the 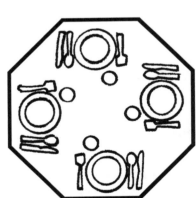s.

Scientist Sam
and the
Marvelous
Shape Machine

A "Read and Trace" Story

1

He turned a knob and
cranked a wheel. Out came
a **circle**—no big deal.

3

Two more turns, a sputter
and a spout. A puff of smoke
and four **squares** came out.

This is Scientist Sam, a brilliant man,
whose Shape Machine is the best ever seen.

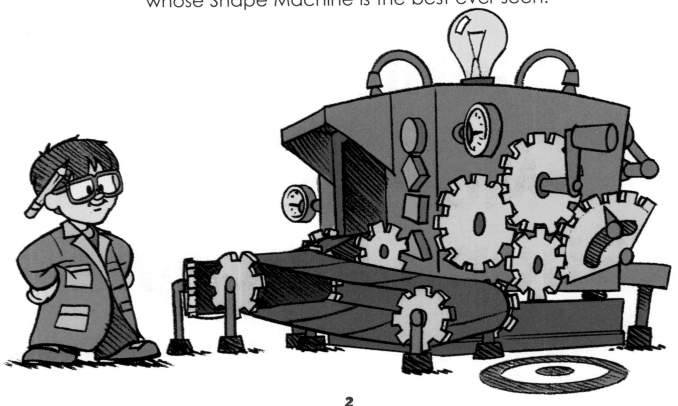

2

Charge the engine! Turn the crank!
A huge **rectangle** appeared.
It looked like a tank.

Slow down the machine. It's starting
to smoke. It spit out a **triangle**.
That's no joke!

4

Scientist Sam gave the machine a
new part. It could make
diamonds right from the start.

5

Suddenly, there was a very loud
sound. A **star** tumbled out
and fell to the ground.

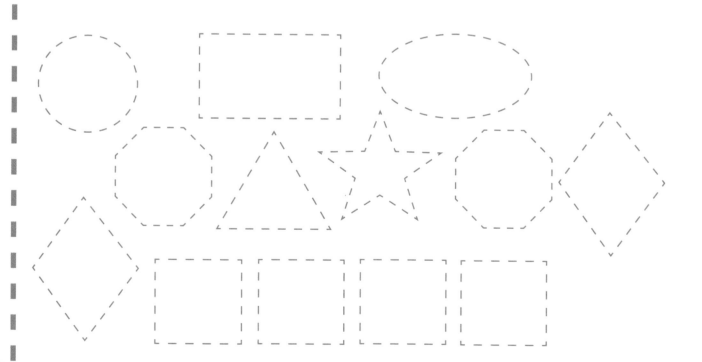

Thirteen different shapes in all
made by Scientist Sam.

7

What will they make?
Could it be a man?

Sparks flew! There was a huge rumble. A large **oval** rolled and fell in a tumble.

The marvelous machine began to work very fast. Out came two **octagons**, the shapes that are last.

6

Scientist Sam says,
"Meet Robot Shape.
He is so super,
he even wears a cape."

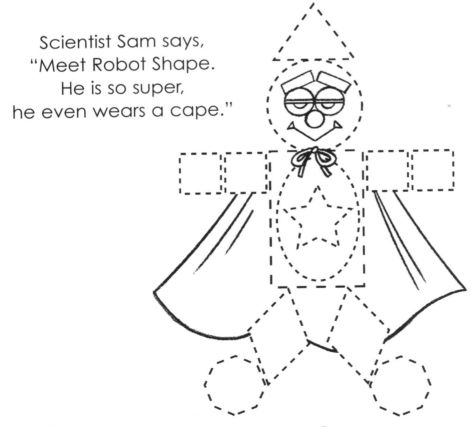

8

Match the Shapes

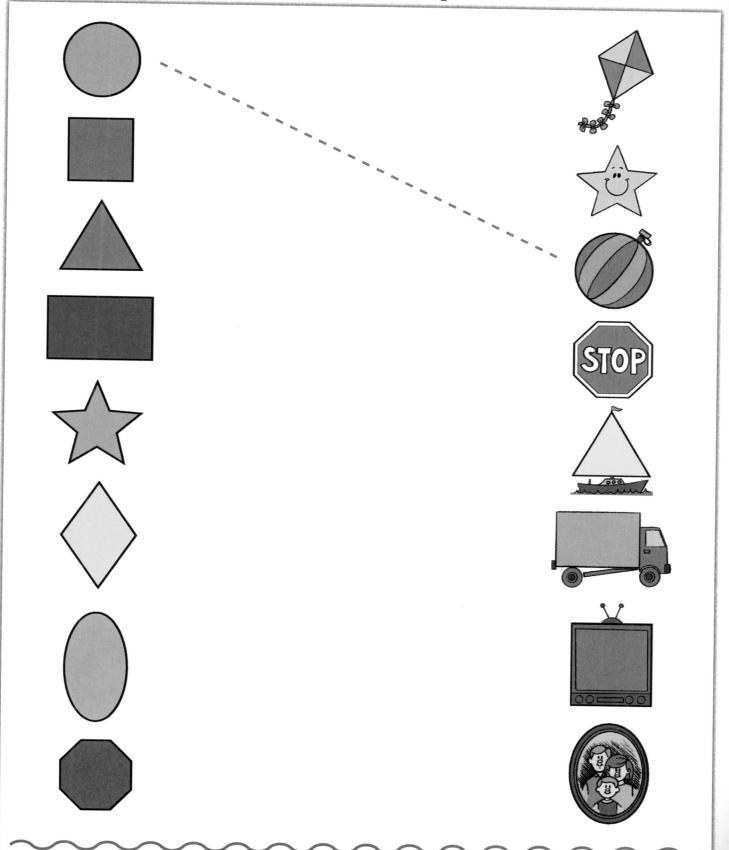

Trace and Color Mr. Shape

MR. SHAPE

TRACE AND COLOR ME!

Animal Puzzle

Cut and paste.
Match each animal head to the correct body.

Awards

 **I know my colors!**

Name: _____ Date: _____

I'm great with shapes!

Name: _____ Date: _____

I know my numbers 1–10!

The ABC's don't trick me!

Name: _____ Date: _____

I love listening to stories!

Name: _____ Date: _____

I know many basic concepts: up, down, on, off, in, out, over, under, and more . . .

Name: _____ Date: _____

I am learning to use a pencil!

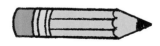

Name: _____ Date: _____

I learned my safety lessons!

Name: _____ Date: _____